Let's Count to 100!

Masayuki Sebe

Kids Can Press

There are 100 mice!
Count them all, starting with the brown ones.

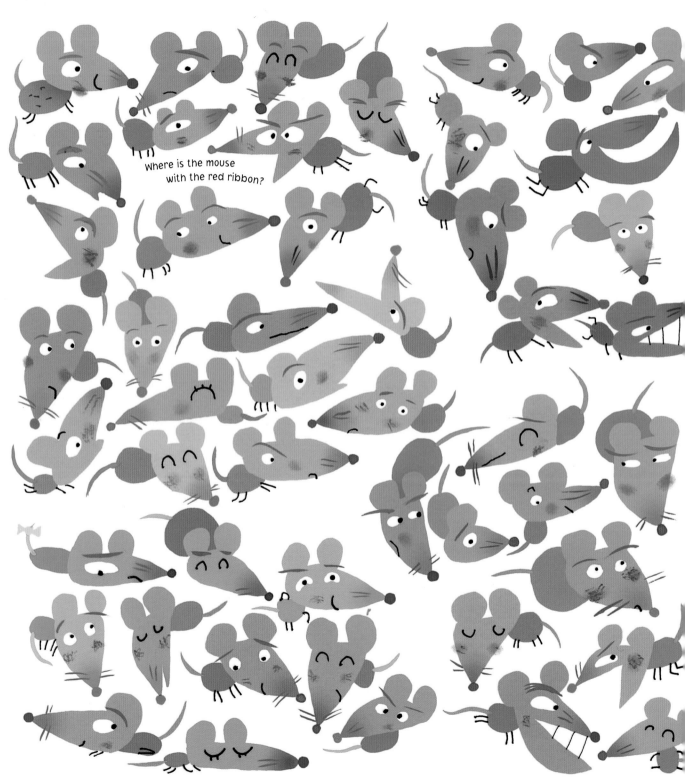

Where is the mouse with the red ribbon?

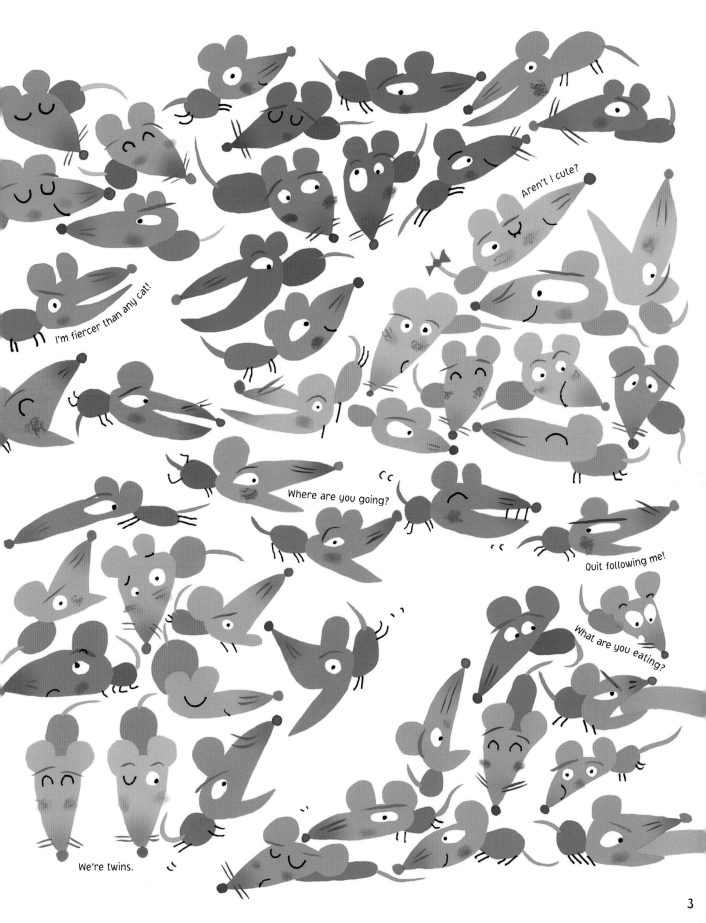

3

There are **100** cats!
How many have striped tails?

Please don't pull my whiskers.

Gotcha!

Hee! That tickles!

4

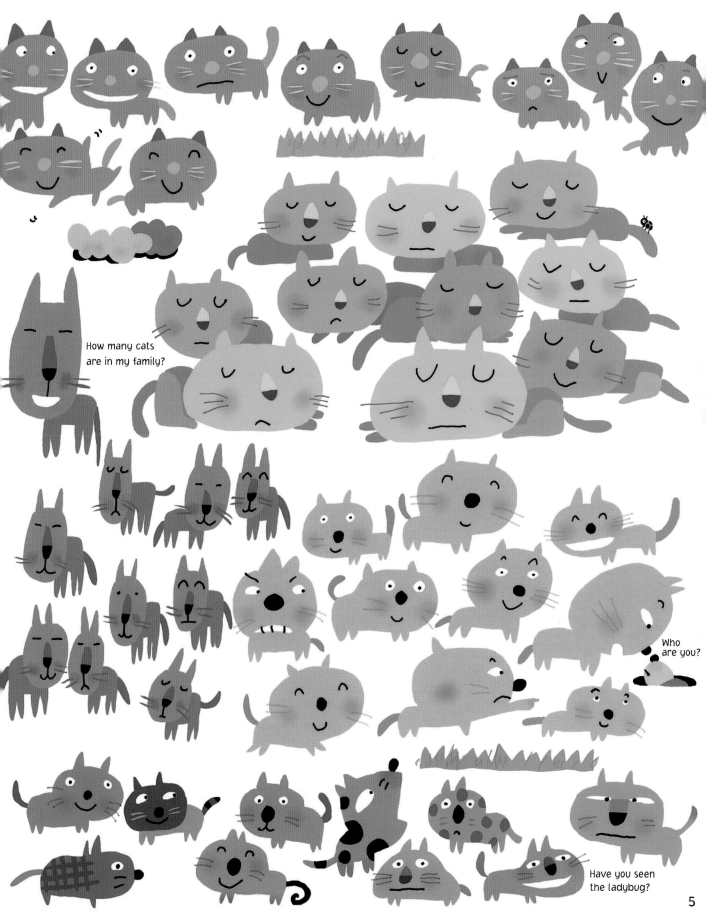

How many cats are in my family?

Who are you?

Have you seen the ladybug?

5

There are **100** moles.

What's that?

I don't want to know!

You stink!

Pee-ew!

Ahh! I feel much better.

I'm digging.

Careful!

6

How many are snuggled up with a frog?

There are **100** sheep ...

and 1 rabbit! (Do you see him?)

There are **100** birds.

Are there enough berries for everyone?

Yum!

I like being upside down.

Got it!

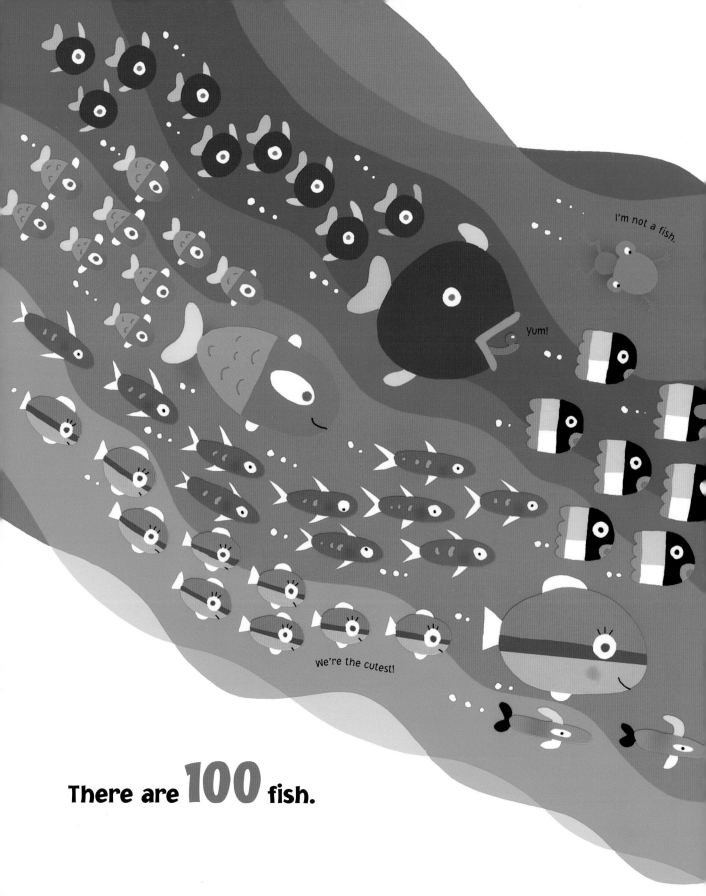

There are **100** fish.

How many different kinds of fish are there?

How many elephants are smiling?

I'm lost.

Ready, set, count!

That looks
tasty!

15

Thank you!

Who likes to play soccer?

There are **100** kids!

Hey!

Who has candy?

How many apples do you see?

Count them all.

17

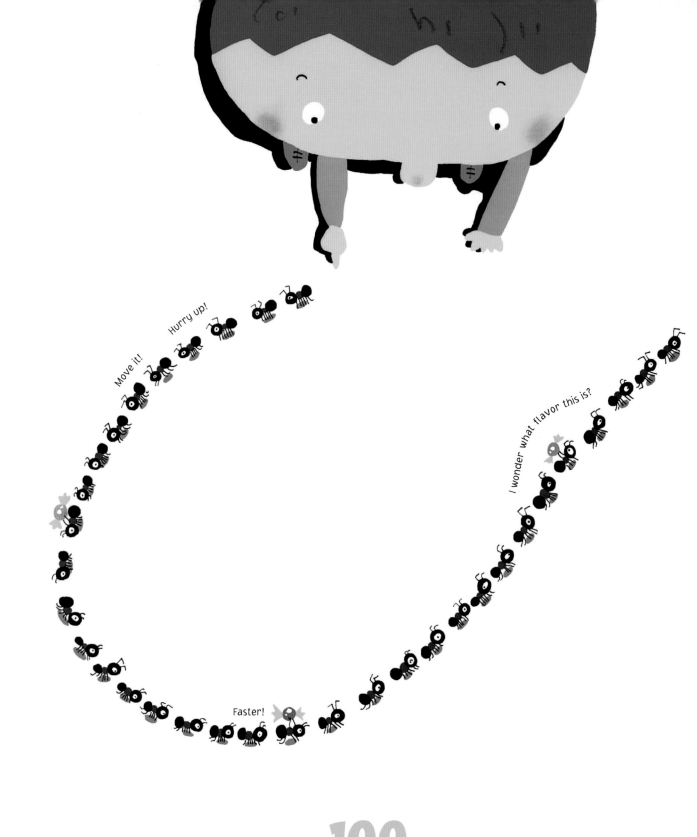

There are 100 ants!

How many are carrying candy?

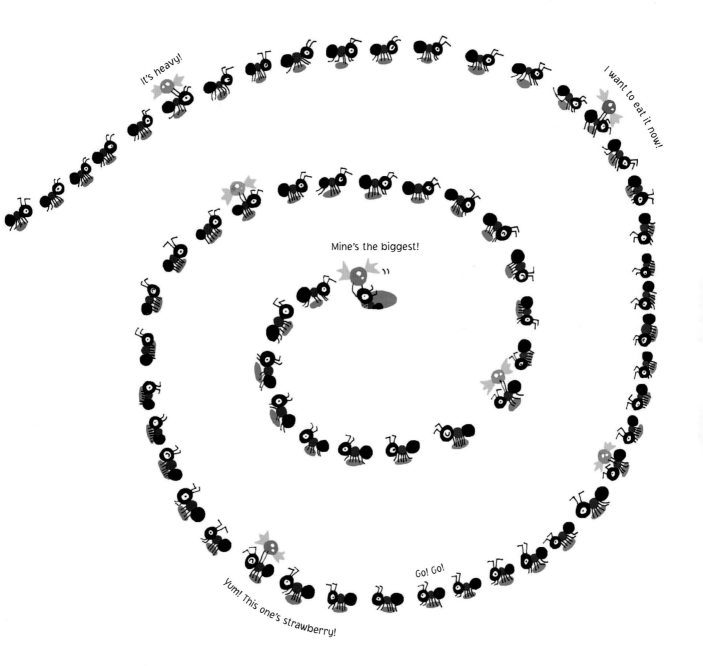

I want a carrot.

Maybe I should play outside.

Where is the mouse?

20

There are **100** cars and trucks!

Beep! Beep!

Woop-woop!

Wee-oo! Wee-oo!

I like watermelon.

And **100** houses!

There are **10** mice, **10** cats, **10** moles, **10** sheep, **10** birds, **10** fish, **10** elephants, **10** kids, **10** ants and **10** houses.

What?

That makes **100** in all!

Tweet!
Tweet!

Meow!

Yikes — a cat!

Go! Go! Go!

Did you see ...

the mouse with the
yellow bow?
(pages 2–3)

this cat?
(pages 4–5)

the farting mole?
(pages 6–7)

the snowman?
(pages 8–9)

this bird?
(pages 10–11)

this frog?
(pages 12–13)

the elephant
holding a pineapple?
(pages 14–15)

who was wearing
this hat?
(pages 16–17)

the girl with a
strawberry on her head?
(pages 16–17)

the boy cuddling this
cat?
(pages 16–17)

this sleeping ant?
(pages 18–19)

the mouse's house?
(pages 20–21)

this house?
(pages 20–21)

this truck?
(pages 20–21)